HAIKU-SINE

HAIKU-SINE

*217 Tiny Food Poems by
Texans Who Love to
Eat & Feed Their Heads*

*Edited by Micki McClelland
Illustrations by Shelby Watson*

LAZYWOOD PRESS
Houston, Texas

• • •

Copyright © 2000 Lazywood Press
All rights reserved. No portion of this book may be reproduced —
mechanically, electronically or by any other means, including photocopying
— without written permission of the publisher.

ISBN 0-9665-7163-0

Editor & publisher: Teresa Byrne-Dodge
Project editor: Micki McClelland
Director of special projects: Paula Murphy
Art director & illustrator: Shelby Watson

Lazywood Press
9337-B Katy Freeway, #271
Houston, Texas 77024

• • •

ACKNOWLEDGEMENTS

Lazywood Press has more nuts than a Mr. Goodbar, and without them this book would never have happened. Thank you, senior editor Micki McClelland, for channeling your quirky imagination into this project. It was Micki who first coined the term haiku-sine. *("Sounds like 'haute cuisine,' get it? Get it? Get it!" she semi-patiently explained.)*

Shelby Watson, thank you for your charm, your delicious drawings, for giving graphic form to our intellectual amusement.

Paula Murphy, our director of special projects, you combine practicality and good taste, artistry and wisdom. All this, and not yet 30!

I'd also like to thank the many, many Texans — most of whom we have never met — who took the time to consider food, tick off the syllables on their fingers and pen the haiku that appear in this book. Bon appétit. Or, as the Japanese say, Hadakaimasu!

— *Teresa Byrne-Dodge, editor & publisher*

PREFACE

In the October-November 1997 issue of *My Table: Houston's Dining Magazine*, we published a call for hungry poets: Write a haiku — the Japanese poetic form of 17 syllables in three lines — with a food theme and perhaps win dinner for four in a Houston Japanese restaurant. We promised to publish the results in our December-January issue and secretly hoped for enough to fill a magazine page.

The response was overwhelming: bulging manila envelopes bearing entries — many of them illustrated — from entire classes of high school and middle school students, emailed haiku from enigmatic cyber-poets, lovely hand-written haiku on elegant social stationery, enthusiastic entries from creative-writing clubs. We had so much fun reading those delectable tidbits that we have repeated the contest every year since.

This book features the best of the first three years of *My Table*'s Haiku-Sine contest, including many entries that we did not have space to publish in the magazine. Additionally, we twisted a few toques and gathered food-themed haiku from Texas chefs, restaurateurs and caterers. Altogether, this book showcases more than 200 haiku from Texans "who love to eat and feed their heads."

INTRODUCTION

Haiku-Sine: 1,240 Years In The Making

DITTIES DIVINE

Haiku began as a game.

Imagine it's Japan 760 AD. Imagine you've wandered over to the emperor's palace, only to find the usual crowd of feudal lords and ladies hanging around looking bored. Suddenly, a man jumps up and recites a perfect 17-syllable poem. Solemnly, he dedicates this wondrous paean to the gods.

Gender and imagination challenged, a gifted poetess then rises to the occasion and answers the man's song with a couplet of 14 syllables. Her poetical voice also soars aloft, for she too is anxious to catch the ears of any deities who might be eavesdropping.

The historical record tells us the Imperial Court was tickled pink, with the emperor himself claiming pre-eminence as the person most delighted. Instantly the songs were ordained *tanka*, defined as the majestically reverent process of linking a 5-7-5-syllable phrase of praise to a 7-7-syllable response in kind.

The inspirational game of verbal volleyball spread throughout the land.

Soon everyone was playing. People were popping up all over the place reciting brief, but picturesque verses. The new poetical form took on the construction of a chain, with the word paintings dubbed *renga*, or linked elegance.

For 900 hundred years, Japanese poets enjoyed royal favor, spouting off their classy *renga* at the drop of a crown. Often inspiration bloated into zeal, and it was not unheard of for some concatenations to be forged of 10,000 links!

COMIC RELIEF

Then, as benefits the way of all flesh, around 1660 the poems evolved (or devolved, depending on one's bend of mind) into comedy. The humorous *hokku* — or starting verse — found popular support among working stiffs, who tend to love the pun more than the pundit.

Leader of the chuckle movement was Matsuo Basho, who had a flair for word play, double entendre, paradox, the verbal pratfall. He was a jolly stickler for "keeping it light," which is the mantra of all great comedians. Regarding *kurumi*, or weightlessness in the haiku, Basho thought verses should be "light as a shallow river flowing over its sandy bed."

Not particularly funny, true, but the recommendation immortalized a place for Basho in the evolution of haiku.

A ROSE BY ANY OTHER NAME

Over the centuries, the poetic form continued to undergo renovation.

Enter Masaoka Shiki. Celebrated as the modern father of the ancient art, Shiki added the elements of curiosity and reality to the whimsical wisp of poetic expression. It was Shiki who pronounced the ultra-formal gods-pandering, emperor-backed *renga* passé.

Then he played around with the words *hokku* and *haikai* (any verse in a *renga*), and invented a modern tag for the ancient discipline. Thus was born, haiku. Shiki loved his own innovation so much, the man wrote 23,000 haiku before he died in 1902 at age 36.

One of the most engaging aspects of Shiki's shtick is referred to as "the haiku moment." If that sounds too much like a beer commercial, think instead of the *"Ah–ha!"* moment, or the point in a haiku when the reader smiles with recognition. Sometimes subtle, sometimes like a blast of cold wind, the *Ah–ha!* is the *attaboy!* of haiku.

Brevity is the soul of this wit. To be quick on the brain, to be nimble with nibbles of words, to write cleverly with adroit observation rather than droning on — this is the soft, sweet underbelly of the successful haiku.

It is also a discipline that asks both the writer and the reader to throw themselves inside the *right now*. Let Shakespeare creep along at the petty pace of "tomorrow and tomorrow and tomorrow." Haiku urge us to catch the quicksilver of the current moment before it vanishes forever.

To accomplish immediacy, Shiki ordained that modern haiku must be strictly limited to songs set in one of the seasons of nature. Alas, it is at this point we take our departure from the master.

Unruly little rule-breaking foodies that we are, the poets of *Haiku-Sine* have made their focus not the seasons, but the seasonings. To skew a famous line of poetry (with apologies to King Solomon), this book suggests "the voice of the turtle soup is heard in the land." And it is food, glorious food, that guides our passion.

— Micki McClelland, editor

QUOTES

"We didn't just read poetry, we let it drip from our tongues."
— Robin Williams in the film, *Dead Poets Society*

"More than inspiration, it needs meditation, effort and mainly perception to compose a real haiku."
— Rodrigo de Siqueira, Chilean poet/artist
(www.insite.com.br/rodrigo/poet/haiku.html)

"Poetry without rules is like a tennis match without a net."
— Robert Frost, American poet (1874-1963)

"Learn the rules; and then forget them."
— Matsuo Basho, Japanese haiku master (1644-1694)

"Haiku should have a reverence for life and living. Haiku has humor — it delights in word play, puns and the comic side of life. It does not use sarcasm to make a point — limericks take care of that."
— Jane Reichhold, haiku scholar/poet

CONTENTS

Zoned Comfort
In the Raw
Fish Stories
Straight Up
Wicked Ways
Food for Thought
Sexy Texy Mexy
Mother Wit & The Inner Child
Down Home
Fast Breaking & The Caffeine Wall
Foreign Affairs
Ancient Grease
Teeth Sinkers & Meaty Issues
Haiku Root
Sweet Dessertions

How brave the chicken
To sacrifice itself for
The commonest cold.

—*Mark Rodriguez, San Antonio*

Hungry pilgrims made
Heaping pots of succotash
Winter's antidote.

—*Keith Fuller, The Woodlands*

Girls' dinner party—
Sun-dried hot tomatoes and
Tough cookies, fab dish.

—*Gail Donohue Storey, Houston*
Haiku-Sine Contest Winner 1999

Brie meets with hot fire
Wrapped in warm arms of phyllo.
Crust breaks, spilling cheese.

—Hayley Hamilton, Dallas

Midnight bedtime snacks —
Raid the refrigerator.
It cannot fight back.

—*Stephen Lemrond, Houston*

My mouth's journey starts
With tastes that capture my heart.
An escape, by plate.

— *Melissa Fowler, Houston*

Chicken noodle soup.
Hunger, colds and sinuses
Do not have a chance.

—*Eric Weiner, Houston*

Sometimes chef Mark Cox
Tops risotto with cream peas —
A freakin' genius.

—Linda Barth, Houston

Dark satin blanket
Tucks the almond into bed,
Lulling me to sleep.

— *Emily Skelton, Houston*

If you love someone
Hold the sugar and flour.
Try kisses instead.

—Joan Ifland Johnson, Houston

A sneer on his lips,
Lambchops meet jelly donuts —
The King finds solace.

— *Marianne Fairey, Houston*

The start of gumbo —
Celery, peppers, onions —
The holy trio.

—*Karen Lerner, A Fare Extraordinaire, Houston*

Once mild milk, a wedge
Of bleu-veined pungence pairs well
With figs or walnuts.

— *Teresa Byrne-Dodge, Houston*

Flounder wrapped in foil
Corn on the cob, smoky grill
Summertime again.

—Anne Smith; Corpus Christi

Harvest meal — apples,
Cider, popcorn, fudge — with the
Scent of falling leaves.

—Patricia Hill, Houston

Football, tailgate meals,
Chrysanthemums in full bloom —
Fall has descended.

—*John C. Yearwood, Woodville*

Mom's chicken-fried steak,
Cream gravy, mashed potatoes.
This is paradise.

—Cathy Rowell, Midlothian

IN THE RAW

Tender artichoke
Reveals its succulent heart
To prying fingers.

—Georgia Terrell, Houston

Pop open pea pods.
Set free some plump round voyeurs —
Peeping toms in green.

—*Jane Butkin Roth, Bellaire*

Slice crisp bell pepper,
Find curly baby within.
Never two the same.

—Ginny Renfroe, Bellaire

Hostess is speechless!
Guest at the cheese tray eats the
Radish mouse garnish.

—*Ann Reisfeld Boutté, Houston*

Homegrown lemons, big
As suns, tumble from their bowl
But find no escape.

—*Keddy Ann Outlaw, Houston*

The sweet, juicy fruit,
Filled with disturbing black seeds,
A delicious treat.

—*Angela Wo, Sugar Land*

Snap some sugar, Peas!
I see your brussels sprouting.
You come from shy greens.

—Jane Butkin Roth, Bellaire

Texan meets Cuban.
Deejay marries NASA boy.
Love is more garlic.

—*Dayna Steele-Justiz, Houston*

Mike Tyson eats ears,
No preservatives added.
Boxing keeps them fresh.

—*Terry Sullivan, Houston*

Raw oyster slips down
My throat like a water slide
Chased by a saltine.

— *Chablis Jokinen, Houston*

Diets are devils.
Carrots, celery, lettuce,
Tools of destruction.

—*Karen Royer, Royers' Round Top Café, Round Top*

Dandy lions crouch
In a ditch beside the road.
Picked, they do not roar.

—*Jake Crimestein, Dime Box*

Desperately lonely,
Talk loud on cell phone, bleating.
Hang up, friend, and eat.

—*Janice Adelle Rossen, Austin*

A grape per raisin
And a plum per every prune.
The fruits watch in awe.

—*Stephen Lemrond, Houston*

FISH STORIES

Lox reminds me of
Salmon-chanted evening where
Bagels dress in pink.

—*David Nathan, Houston*
Haiku-Sine Contest Winner 1997

I crave fried catfish —
Whole, hot, crunchy, Tabasco'd.
Whiskery blessing!

— Howard Peacock, Woodville

A pint of Guinness
To wash down the fish and chips —
My redhead's request.

—*Marianne Fairey, Houston*

Buttery, nutty
Favorite flaky white fish —
Bet your sweet sea bass.

—Joe Martinez, Riviera Grill, Houston

Scram for clam chowder —
New England's greatest power
To stop the chatter.

—*Jeremy Kowis, Houston*

Exercise is said
To put muscle in your head.
Bivalves work for me.

—*Eric L. Dodge, Houston*

Watching Uncle Bob
Eat fish cheeks in Canada,
A complete turn-off.

—*Chablis Jokinen, Houston*

Foodies see seafood
Even in their dreams. Fish dream
Of foodies — See food!

—*Gail Donohue Storey, Houston*

Our night of pink food —
Sparkling rosé, boiled shrimp
And cotton candy.

—*Jake Crimestein, Dime Box*

Treasures in a shell,
Seafood, tomato, garlic:
Vongole cozze.

—*Lori Farris, Arcodoro, Dallas*

Red muddy creatures,
Little spiders of the pond.
Spicy, tasty bugs.

— *Tara Combs, Houston*

Oysters' orisons—
Acolytes lounge 'neath nude moons
Salty tides for tongues.

—Robert Del Grande, Cafe Annie, Houston

STRAIGHT UP

Like my olives stoned,
Martinis cold to the bone,
Always together.

—*Eric L. Dodge, Houston*

Sapphire shining bright,
Drowning olive eyeballs wink.
Night eclipses day.

—Christine Cole, Houston

White creamy water,
Five dollars a cup Dome foam.
Get your ice cold beer!

— *Blake Ragland, Houston*

Primping in wood kegs
until the wine is mature:
Great legs, lovely nose.

—*Lora Pelton, Houston*

Late in the evening
Memories of the day past.
Tequila sunrise.

—*Michael R. Childers, Houston*

Cheek piercing, teeth sting —
Ah, tequila mockingbird!
Lime literacy.

—Dawn Marie Cole, Houston

Meet at the bar, where
A Campari and soda
Begins our dinner.

— *Lori Farris, Pomodoro, Dallas*

Creaky crack flip-top,
Pristine pip pop — steamy chill,
Foamy cream cascade.

—Amy Fontinelle, Houston

Chipotle pepper
In my vodka martini.
What a disaster.

—*Chris Castellani, Houston*

Glass of wine. With that
He asks nonchalantly of
My nerves and bad hair.

—*Jennifer Hubbs & Jennifer Sanders, Houston*

Cheap scotch, Boone's Farm, beer —
Dating when young, in college.
Thank God I'm thirty.

—Hayley Hamilton, Dallas

Irish whiskey burns
Tongue, throat, gut and all ten toes.
Pour me another.

—*Teresa Byrne-Dodge, Houston*

Love juice, yeasty love.
Sierra Nevada spews
Froth drips to my lips.

— *Shannon Wynne, 8.0 & The Flying Saucer, Dallas*

Red and white held high,
Laughing, eating, toasting friends.
Cheeks flushed, heart of life.

—*Kathleen Laborde, San Antonio*

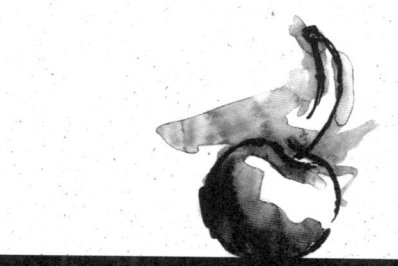

WICKED WAYS

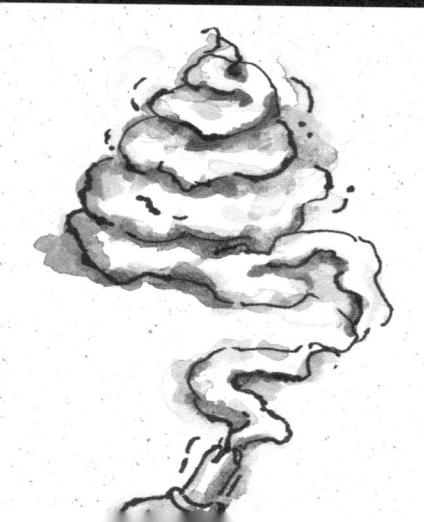

Lingering over
Dinner, two old friends become
Lovers entangled.

—*Bill Stephens, San Antonio*

Symbol of teachers,
The repellent of doctors,
The red fruit of sin.

—*Roatha Chap, Houston*

Best I ever had,
Said the man to his new bride,
Tasting her cooking.

—*Charlene Turner, Houston*

Love on the half shell:
Eighteen ways to tickle luck,
A night of romance.

—*Perry Andersson, McCormick & Schmick's, Houston*

The artichoke whole
Hides tender heart under pricks.
In my bed, the same.

— *Micki McClelland, Houston*

Food for the body
So tempting to the spirit.
The table is set.

— *Tom Farrar, Houston*

That first night you said
Breadcrumbs clung to my black shirt
Like stars for our sky.

—*Jane Butkin Roth, Bellaire*

Red hot cherry pie —
Your juices flow all over.
I want to eat you.

—*Chris Dauterive, Houston*

Flavor symphony
Best shared with friends and lovers,
Touching tongues and hearts.

— *Charlene Turner, Houston*

To motivate me,
He will watch my kitchen work.
O my love, eggs on.

—*Micki McClelland, Houston*

First time that we kiss,
My own sweet peaches and cream,
Magnificent dream.

—*Claudia Vu, Houston*

The kitchen is his
For creating her dinner —
Eaten together.

—*Carol Lee, Houston*

I smell your garden
Simmering in my soup bowl.
I taste your passion.

—*L.Z. Martini, Houston*

Boyfriends and brownies,
Two things that never last long.
I eat them both up.

— *Nancy Sarnoff, Houston*

Calories swimming
In tempting rich chocolate.
Swim to me, baby!

—*Karen Royer, Royers' Round Top Café, Round Top*

FOOD FOR THOUGHT

Focusing on life,
Slowly I fold the batter.
Complex made simple.

— *Andrew Forrest, Houston*

You are what you eat.
You eat what tastes delicious.
You are delicious.

—*Micki McClelland, Houston*

The earth's finest fruits,
Prepared by hands creative,
Are almost holy.

—*Charlene Turner, Houston*

Preparing a meal
A third trip to the market.
Shopping wise, the key.

—*Ernie Manouse, Houston*

Tea leaves in a pot
Float green as lover's imprint.
Melt, feed me fortunes.

—*Jane Butkin Roth, Bellaire*

Vegetarians
Lust not for tofu, greens — but
Chocolate and champagne.

—*Gail Donohue Storey, Houston*

Wise chefs say: Only
Fools rush in baking soufflés,
'cause they'll fall on you.

— *Kimberly Jordan, Houston*

Potato chipping
The onion dip is like life.
You can't get enough.

— Jake Crimestein, Dime Box

Fire ants, candied ants —
Ants that bite, ants that you bite —
A picnic for both.

— *Nathaniel Ngo, Sugar Land*

Gene-altered veggies
Served by jellyfish's glow?
Let's trust the old ways.

— *Bruce Auden, Biga on the Banks, San Antonio*

Onions boiled tender
Turn crystalline, convert sweet.
Alchemy, my dear.

—*Ginny Renfroe, Bellaire*

CNN, Fox News,
MSNBC, Dateline...
The family meal.

—Hayley Hamilton, Dallas

Make reservations,
A favorite for dinner.
Now that's a good cook.

—*Kelly Horst, Fort Worth*

Count the sunny hours.
Live your life to its fullest.
Call a friend, eat out!

—John C. Yearwood, Woodville

Emu for the boots,
Ostrich for the belt and hat.
Don't eat'em, wear'em.

—*Sally Jennifer Cody, Blanco*

You are a good egg,
Halo bouncing off your shell,
Golden heart inside.

—*Shelby Watson, Houston*

SEXY TEXY MEXY

Grab salsa and cheese
In queso emergency.
Come on, light my fire.

— *David Henry, Bellaire*

Cilantro and cheese
Enchiladas — onions piled.
Hangovers napped off.

—*Mark Rodriguez, San Antonio*

A crimson pepper —
Raw fuse focusing white heat,
Brow-born beads of sweat.

—*Page W. Benway, Houston*

Mole chocolate
Melting spicy — ancient kiss,
Mayan reminisce.

—Erica Hernandez, Houston

A margarita
And chicken in tortilla.
Glad señorita!

—*Lora Pelton, Houston*

Chili is best hot.
My dad makes it with beer, but
There's nothing to fear.

—*Matthew Millik, Houston*

Love homegrown eating?
With picante, tortillas?
Tex-Mex is all corn.

—*Micki McClelland, Houston*

Spicy hot salsa,
Surprise party in your mouth.
Chips scratch down your throat.

—Allison Nitsch & Michelle Buchta, Spring

Y'all like spicery
Be it chili, salsa, beans.
State of the state — hot.

—*Ernie Manouse, Houston*

Basket on table
Long ago bereft of chips —
Waiter on smoke break.

—Tim Brookover, Houston

Avocado dies
In the blades of the blender.
Guacamole's born.

—Paige Robinson, Houston

MOTHER WIT & THE INNER CHILD

Sippy cup of milk,
Oreos with two teeth marks,
Waiting for Santa.

— *Marianne Fairey, Houston*

Backyard barbecue —
Homemade burgers ā la Dad.
"Kiss the Cook" apron.

—Quinn Corte, Bellaire

Olives on fingers —
Peanuts, raisins up the nose.
Eating was child's play.

—*Jane Butkin Roth, Bellaire*

Dewberry cobbler —
One taste and I'm with Granny
Peavy in heaven.

—*Linda Barth, Houston*

Frosted graham cracker,
Grape juice and Jesus — Sunday
School special. Soul food.

—*Chablis Jokinen, Houston*

When Noah turned one —
Frosted hands, chocolate face,
Delighted in cake.

—*Malia Messina, Houston*

Large white sticky fun,
Topped with sports, action heroes —
The boy's birthday cake.

—Jared Flynn, Houston

Lions, tigers, bears—
All of them in my big mouth.
Where is Dorothy?

—*Tim Boughal, Sugar Land*

Mother's warm cookies,
A soft and fragrant refuge,
Leave me wanting more.

—*Adam Epstein, Houston*

Burned black and crispy,
Pepper mountains, tons of salt —
My daddy's cooking.

—*Ellen Currie, Houston*

Squash, beets, spinach, too
Multiplying on a plate.
A child's worst nightmare.

—*Kathy Black, Cypress*

Pizza, stew or beans,
TV trays, remote control —
Tuesday at Dad's house.

—Laura Elder, Houston

Glop of puréed corn —
Saltines smashed to smithereens.
Highchair, low manners.

—*Jake Crimestein, Dime Box*

Mom's grasshopper pie,
Mint cream pond with cookie shore.
All insects were spared.

—*David C. Newell, Houston*

Nobody cooks like
My mother. Not even the
World's best chefs compare.

—*Carol Lee, Houston*

Piano music.
Mother sings loud the old songs.
She plays with her food.

—*Susanne R. Bowers, Houston*

My mother, eighty,
Still finds spaghetti daring.
Health food too risky.

—*Ginny Renfroe, Bellaire*

DOWN HOME

Collard — sweet green weed —
Marries fatback, Papa's dream.
Summer's music steams.

—*J. Scott McCleery*, Houston

Grits, smooth perfection —
Just add bacon and butter
True Southern comfort.

—*Tom Williams, Fox Diner, Houston*

Golden brown turkey,
Buttery mashed potatoes,
Stuffing stuffing you.

—*Sara Wrye, Houston*

A mouthful of sun,
Warm sunlight embraced by spice.
Then it descended.

—Barbara Bartsch-Allen, Houston

Piping hot cherries,
A snowball of milk atop.
American pie!

—*Brendan Kennedy, Houston*

Fearlessly flaming,
Choking, smoking toque on fire —
Jeff's not shooting Blanks.

—*Jeff Blank, Hudson's on the Bend, Austin*

Texas menus do
List macaroni and cheese
As vegetables.

— *Shirley Redwine, Houston*

Barnyard fried chicken,
Cream gravy, okra, corn, beans —
Blue plate, 1910.

—Hayley Hamilton, Dallas

Spiny red mudbugs
Yield spicy tender tidbits —
Big Easy popcorn.

—*Ann Reisfeld Boutté, Houston*

Picking blueberries
We came home with purple arms —
Faces brimming spring.

—*Keddy Ann Outlaw, Houston*

If you have to ask:
"Hey, you guys, what is a grit?"
You're not from Texas.

—Shirley Redwine, Houston

Snowing parmesan,
Noodles twisting around fork —
My spaghetti night.

—*Laura Elder, Houston*

Pink honey-baked ham,
Holiday gift or insult?
Pig's butt no excuse.

—*Teresa Byrne-Dodge, Houston*

Chitlins' odors make
The yard dogs whimper and dance,
Stomachs crying tears.

—*J. Scott McCleery, Houston*

Luckenbach, Texas
With Willie, Waylon, *et al*.
Al drank all the beer.

— *Albert Grumbakker, Fredericksburg*

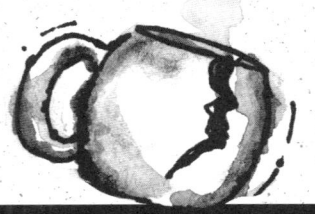

FAST BREAKING & THE CAFFEINE WALL

Dancing beetle beans,
Rainforest in my kitchen.
Hava java cup.

—*Judith Monroe, Sugar Land*

Chocolate latte
Mocha grande diet for two,
Climb the caffeine wall.

—*Jennifer Hubbs & Jennifer Sanders, Houston*

Hot fat cream gravy,
Pepper streaking, cheese reeking.
Run, yellow yolk, run!

—Howard Peacock, Woodville

I'm hyperactive,
Nervous as a whore in church.
Blame it on Starbucks.

—*Wayne Ledford, Houston*

Onion, blueberry,
Or rye — a bag of bagels.
Breakfast food to go.

—*Robert Dunigan, Sugar Land*

Coffee pot pumping,
The bacon sizzles and squirms —
Eggs' first paramours.

—Joe Abuso, Abuso Catering Co., Houston

Corn flakes wake me up.
Chamomile tea makes me sleep.
Restaurant for lunch.

—*Ken Davis, Sugar Land*

Black as my burnt toast.
Take a sip, I'm on my way.
Lightning in a cup.

—*Alison Kouba, Houston*

Two eggs and bacon
On flat bread, arranged to make
Kids glow. Smiley face.

—Holly McFarland, Houston

Liquid in a shell.
Break it, watch the yellow yolk
Flow out the thin crack.

—*Erica Krueger, Houston*

Are they not the same?
Rice Crispies versus Crisp Rice —
Taste is in the name.

—*Anna Iriemi, Houston*

A pot of green tea
Tastes like rustified water.
Coffee is better.

—*Joe Abuso, Abuso Catering Co., Houston*

Fresh café au lait,
Beignets dusted with sugar:
French Quarter sunrise.

—*Ann Reisfeld Boutté, Houston*

Decaf espresso,
Jamaican mocha latte.
What happened to Joe?

—*Brian Marr, Houston*

Breakfast on a plane.
I shrink from its old fruit and
Stale bread. Hungry flight.

—*Jennifer Hubbs & Jennifer Sanders, Houston*

That four o'clock wave,
Craving for a caffeine fix.
Coffee is my junk.

—*Wayne Ledford, Houston*

Hotel corned beef hash,
Poach two, side of cottage fries —
Eaten at bed's edge.

—Mark Rodriguez, San Antonio

Omelet, scrambled, poached —
Eggs are eaten every way
You can imagine.

— *Nikki Kasmai, Houston*

First smoke at thirteen —
First cup of coffee, age eight.
Stomach gone to hell.

—*Jake Crimestein, Dime Box*

Dawn, smoking coffee.
Pillowed porch rocker, soft rain.
I sip day's first light.

—*Howard Peacock, Woodville*

FOREIGN AFFAIRS

Crispy fries of France,
Distinguished from other spuds
By golden panache.

—*David C. Newell, Houston*

Dreams of her kugel
And my Bubbe's blintz soufflé.
Knish dream be true?

—*Jane Butkin Roth, Bellaire*

Hail, mighty Caesar,
Garlicky salad hero!
Crunch, noble crouton.

—*Shirley Barr, Houston*

GrAPES, IOX, LLAMA beans,
asBEARagus, BULLogna:
A cook's safari.

—Ann Reisfeld Boutté, Houston

If you had one wish,
Would it be for world peace? Nah,
Make fried foods healthful.

—*Linda Barth, Houston*

Set on silver tray,
Rectangled slab of foie gras
Studded with truffles.

—*George Leake, Houston*

Take sips of vino
With an aged parmigiano,
But don't breathe a word.

—*Rosemary French, Austin*

Pasta — ancient as
My cultural ancestors —
Both inside of me.

—*Angela Furman, Houston*

Lamb scrambled with spice —
Tumeric and cardamom
To curry favor.

—*Micki McClelland, Houston*

The Russians love beets
Cooked in a pot with cabbage.
Vodka up keeps down.

—*Jake Crimestein, Dime Box*

Irish soda bread
Thick with raisins, the only
Sign we were Irish.

—*Kennedy Ann Outlaw, Houston*

Frog legs, cabrito,
Menudo, alligator
Don't taste like chicken.

—*Jane Butkin Roth, Bellaire*

Spaetzle and pork roast —
Irma's German heritage
Influences mine.

—*Trish Morille, Houston*

Escargot is snail.
I felt I needed to warn
In case your nose fails.

—*Andrew Harper, Houston*

Mama's prodigy,
Passions run too hot, too cold,
An Italian chef.

—*Lori Farris, Arcodoro, Houston*

ANCIENT GREASE

Lettuce, tomatoes,
Sesame bun, juicy meat.
Cooked well? Rarely done.

—*Holly Mills, Sugar Land*

Ancient grease to fry
Burgers patted pancake thin —
Steel buns, happy meal.

—*Jake Crimestein, Dime Box*

Crisp, crunchy cheese fry
Sitting with his family,
Leaving for my mouth.

—Jonas Herd, Houston

Oven-fresh pizza
Dripping with warm cheese and sauce
Is delivered now.

—*Wes Mock, Sugar Land*

Spicy, drippy cheese
Atop somewhat sodden chips.
Astrodome's purpose.

—*Billy Hesser, Sugar Land*

Pepperoni pond.
Jump from lily to lily,
Finish the last bite.

—*Allison McMullen, Spring*

In all your wisdom,
Please crown me the Sausage King,
Goddess of Pizza!

—*James Boyer, Spring*

Hairnets aplenty,
The golden arches gleaming.
Super-size me, please.

—*Tommy Schulte, Houston*

Popcorn with butter,
Movie food for you and me.
Large Coke makes me go.

—*Armin Federico, Houston*

I like to talk thin,
But I prefer to eat fat.
Double cheeseburger.

—*Chris Tripoli, Houston*

What are you made of?
Your cryptic birth confuses.
Hot dogs are not frank.

—*Riley Kilmer, Houston*

Tempting aroma —
Dripping cheese, red sauce, warm bread.
Why ration passion?

—*Annie Blaylock, Houston*

Hot-as-hell fried spuds!
My tongue seared, breathing labored,
Forehead sweats. Pure bliss.

—*Melissa Vossmer, San Antonio*

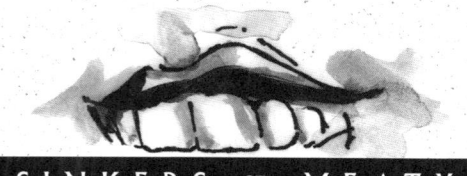

TEETH SINKERS & MEATY ISSUES

Wolf it down, pig out,
Eat like a horse or buzzard —
Whale-sized appetite.

—Jake Crimestein, Dime Box

Slow-cooked shanks of veal —
    Oh, oh so osso buco.
    We don't call it stew.

—Frank Triola, Azzarelli's, Houston

Dinner partners feast
On elk, duck, venison, goose.
Yet, are rarely boared.

—*Dick Dace, Houston*

Oh! You mighty roast,
Full of delectable juice.
Soon you and I... meat?

—*Karl Trollinger, Houston*

God's snail, roly slug —
Riding garlic-parslied swales,
Kissed by angel lips.

—*J. Scott McCleery, Houston*

Eat hearty! Tip well!
Next day, try to remember,
Where's the doggie bag?

— *Sidonia Rose Dick, Spring*

I look in the fridge,
Emptiness is all I find.
All the shops are closed.

—Elizabeth Fischer, Houston

Should I be concerned
That this can of corned beef hash
Smells just like cat food?

—*Teresa Byrne-Dodge, Houston*

Don't eat animals!
(The exception is turkey.)
Happy Thanksgiving.

—Juan Caudillo, Houston

I can't eat a cow
Or any product from it.
Ranchers must hate me.

—*Matt Miller, Houston*

Steak tartar for one,
Raw truth with an egg on top —
Lunch for a skeptic.

— *Micki McClelland, Houston*

HAIKU ROOT

It may be a crime,
But I just love that raw fish.
Don't sue me — sushi.

—Davis Mason, Bellaire

Flimsy sticks waiver,
My fingers tremble and cramp.
The art of chopsticks.

—*Tahira Saleem, Sugar Land*

Crunchy cucumber,
Crab and soft avocado.
California roll.

—Jessica Trincanello, Houston

Greasy noodles and
MSG, sticks for forks and
Message with a treat.

—*Peddy Tabatabai, Houston*

Spring roll or eggroll?
Wonton soup? Hot and sour?
So many choices.

—*Daniel West, Houston*

Onions, folded green,
Shabu-shabu sizzling hot,
Ginger vapor dream.

—*Jane Poole, Houston*

Should Sue sell sushi
By the seashore? Sure, she should
Sell sushi, and shall.

—*Graham Gemoets, Houston*

A sauce of oil-spill,
A slice of polluted sea —
Cramps from the raw truth.

—*Jake Crimestein, Dime Box*

Noodles on my brain,
Prawns, curry, khao soi, thaispice.
Chopsticks from the heart.

—*Annie Wong, Liberty Noodles, Dallas & Houston*

SWEET DESSERTIONS

Pie in the window.
Crispy, golden crust its cell.
Pumpkin prisoner.

—*Lori Goldman, Houston*
Haiku-Sine Contest Winner 1998

I filled up on bread.
I was stuffed by the entrée.
Still had room for cake.

—*Benjamin Mize, Houston*

Twice the sweetened lard.
Who cares about the cookie?
DoubleStuf heaven.

—Paige DiMaggio, Houston

Chocolate lava!
Tiny white marshmallow rafts.
Good hot chocolate.

—*Laura Grest, Fleming Hudrick & Levi Dein, Houston*

Creamy concoction —
Cow juice in three sweet flavors
In tall, frosty glass.

—Christina Fu, Houston

There goes the cherry,
Passing the ice cream mountain —
Going, going, gone.

—*Amy Higgins, Sugar Land*

Creamy cold ice cream
Evokes sensual visions
Of satins and silks.

—Lorraine Yearwood, Woodville

Bittersweet chocolate
Is always best wrapped around
Toasted hazelnuts.

—Gigi Tindall, College Station

Bananas Foster
Lasciviously inflamed,
A flash in the pan.

—*Paula Murphy, Houston*

Gooey chocolate
Mississippi mud cake with
Nuts and marshmallows.

—*Frank Lin, Spring*

Eat we did of pie,
Without fork or cutting knife.
Tongues slurping cherries.

—*Jennifer Kerwin, Fort Worth*

Chewy marshmallows:
The air devours sweet clouds.
I become the air.

—Donna Coyle, Houston

How swell, what a smell —
A cool, whipped, creamy Blue Bell.
Oh hell, my scoop fell.

—*Phillip Anderson, Houston*

Chocolate cream pie —
A minute of pleasure or
A month of regret?

—*Hayley Hamilton, Dallas*

Waistline widening.
No more between-meal snacking.
Curse you, Tootsie Roll!

—*David C. Newell, Houston*

Sour cream raisin
Pie's sugared foam breaks, bakes gold.
Nana's legacy.

— *Melissa Vossmer, San Antonio*

Velvet rich, creamy,
Hot, warm or cold: You delight
Our soul, chocolate.

— *Alexandra Moscovich, Houston*

Jubileed cherries,
Fostered bananas and popped
Lollies. Word candy.

—Micki McClelland, Houston